Deliver I

Based upon a real life e

Author: Jason Love (2015)

Prelude

On October 5th, 1992, sixteen year old Jason Love, an amateur paranormal investigator, agreed to investigate a local house haunting. He was soon engaged in a battle for his own life, as he struggled to protect a family from a powerful, demonic force, intent on killing everyone inside the home.

Today Jason, 40, is an internationally renowned Demonologist, and an expert in violent house haunting. He gives lectures around the world, and still investigates incidents of demonic attacks. He currently lives in Glasgow, Scotland.

Chapter History

Chapter One: Childhood Memories

1987

I was a typical twelve year old kid doing the usual playful activities one would expect. I lived in a small housing estate, just outside the city of Glasgow in Scotland. My parents were professionals in their own fields, and, having a younger brother and sister, our household was always busy and noisy. I was not one for sports, or for that matter, any form of social interaction with others. I enjoyed hanging out with my few friends, staying over at each other's houses, and playing video games on my Sinclair ZX Spectrum.

There was never much on television with regards to the paranormal or ghost haunting in the 1980s. Plenty of slash/ gore movies on VHS video, but nothing in comparison to what we have on the small screen today. I had always been curious about ghosts, as far back as I can remember. My late grandmother had been a sensitive, and would always tell me stories about haunted places she had visited when she was young. This, probably, was the starting stone to my future calling.

The first time I saw a ghost was just after my thirteenth birthday. I was messing about with a friend from school at an old abandoned mental hospital, not far from where I lived. We were not actually inside the building, but hanging around the grassy grounds surrounding the massive property. To be honest, we were up to no good. The idea of chucking stones at the windows seemed fantastic at the time. As I was gathering ammunition ready for my next attack, I caught something out of the corner of my eye. I wasn't sure what it was at first, but as I stood up straight, I stared towards a window on the third floor. It was dark, no curtains or blinds, but I suddenly felt very uneasy as I concentrated my vision on this window.

Suddenly, for just a glimpse of a second, I witnessed a figure appear at the window. It was an old woman. I recall noting the long, grey hair, the aging facial features, and what looked like an old nurse's uniform. I was struck dumb. I remember feeling frozen in time. I couldn't move a muscle. My eyes just stared at this spectacle with fear and terror. My mate Jonathon suddenly threw a pebble at me, hitting my right shoulder. The impact of the assault brought me back to reality. I looked over at my friend, then back towards the window, but nothing. The apparition had vanished. I stuttered slightly as I tried to recall my experience to Jonathon, who quickly diminished my words with laughter and sniggering. What do you expect? Who's really going to believe a teenage boy? Seriously.

I remember re-telling my story to my grandmother a few days after the event. She knew what I was saying was true, and - even though parents and grandparents tend to agree with their children, even if the story is untrue - my grandmother knew, from the way I told it and my bodily reactions, that I was telling the truth. I was scared.

It was at about this time in my young life that I began to accept and to appreciate that there were such things as ghosts and spirits. I learned a lot from my grandmother. She taught me how to open my mind, relax my body, and focus on my spiritual awareness. As time went on, I was taught how to train my third eye, to raise my vibrational level to a higher degree, and to interact with those on the spiritual realm. I am not, and will never claim to be, a psychic or medium. I am, as my grandmother was, a sensitive. I connect with the spiritual world on an emotional level. I can see ghosts and apparitions just as much as anyone else, however, I do have that extra ability to communicate and interact with a spirit, just by being in their presence. This, I suppose, has been a blessing in my modern day role as a Demonologist. I can 'sense' things, either positive or negative, and I can very quickly determine if the presence near me is of demonic or highly negative influence.

My parents didn't really believe in the paranormal, not like my grandmother. They passed it off as being just another 'phase' I was going through. As I spent more time in the company of my grandmother, I learned new tales each time, spurring my imagination, and fuelling my deeper interest in the vast, undiscovered world of the supernatural.

Dark, demonic entities and violent poltergeist cases never interested me at the time. I only knew of, and heard stories about, kind spirits and residual hauntings. This, in turn, would be my downfall in later life.

By 1990, at the ripe old age of 14 (!), I had amassed a huge knowledge base on the paranormal. I even had case files made up in my bedroom, documenting each known entity or supernatural force. I suppose in a way, I was acting out as Fox Mulder from the hit TV show, The X Files. Yeah, OK, I'm a fan of the X Files, but don't hold that against me.

1992. The year I left secondary school, I started hanging out with some boys I had befriended at my local church youth group. We hung out in the evenings, talked football, girls - typical boy chat. Then I discovered they were all huge fans of the paranormal.

Nick, John and Peter, my good friends. We were all roughly the same age group; fifteen, sixteen. Nick and John were both apprentices at a local garage, whilst Peter had a part time job in a dairy float. We would always make jokes at Peter, as he would normally be asleep by 9pm each night. He was awake and out to work at 4am each morning, delivering bottles of milk to customer's door steps.

I, on the other hand, managed to secure myself an apprenticeship with a local Funeral Home. My future career? A bloody undertaker?! The four of us worked hard during daylight hours, but we made up for it in the evenings. None of us touched alcohol or tobacco - perfect boy scouts! We took turns at staying over at each other's homes. We played video games, board games and talked ghosts. Then, one evening, John came up with an idea. The idea of starting up our own ghost hunting group.

Chapter Two: Teenage Ghostbusters

We decided from the start, as a group, to name our club Glasgow Ghost Hunters (GGH). It was primitive, I know, but to a bunch of mid-teens, it was exciting. We didn't have any high tech gear like today's professional groups. A 35mm spool Kodak camera and a cassette voice recorder – one of the one's that hiss terribly when you play back your recordings. That was it!

Armed with our camera and recorder, plus loads of high-beam torches, pencils and a notebook, we were ready for battle.

All we needed now was some 'real' cases of ghostly activity.

Summer of 1992, I got a phone call at my parent's house from a member of the church youth group. George was one of the youth ministers who looked after the under 18's on a Monday and Wednesday evenings. I knew him well, and confided in him with regards to my ghost hunting interests. He spoke with me on the phone, and explained that he felt there was a presence in the church hall. He didn't claim there was a ghost, or anything unnatural, but he did feel that something may be lurking about, and would I be interested in 'investigating' it?

Naturally I was excited at this breaking news, and quickly agreed to undertake the case as soon as possible. We ended our conversation, and after a nod from my mother to use her telephone, I rang my associates from the club. Each one was just as excited as the other after receiving the news. We all agreed to meet up at my place the following Friday evening and thereafter head over to the church hall.

It was a warm but windy Friday night when the four of us arrived at the entrance to the church hall. We stood outside, checking and re-checking our equipment. Rubbing our hands together and pulling on our baseball caps, we entered the back door to the grand hall of St Michael's Church. It was dimly lit by a few half burnt candles. Nick flipped on his torch light and began surveying the area. Peter and I sat down on a bench and opened the equipment bag, pulling out the odds and ends. John was last to enter the hall, and quietly closed the heavy oak door.

We began our investigation by separating into pairs. I took the altar and adjoining rooms along with Peter, Nick explored the upper balcony and organ, whilst John took photos of the large oil paintings that hung along the corridor walls.

In all, we spent the better half of three hours at our first investigation. Our photos, which took four days to process, came back with a few Orbs and some white mist. We were delighted with our discovery and factual evidence. The tape recorder only picked up Nick's farting in the distance, and sniggering from the rest, but nothing much else.

We felt successful! This was our first case investigation for GGH.

Over the following 6 weeks, the four of us investigated around a dozen cases. Nothing truly exciting to be honest. We explored graveyards, churches, old abandoned hospitals and a former nineteenth century prison, long closed down. Our evidence generally consisted of Orbs and strange mists, a few suspect dark shadows, but that was about it.

By late summer, our group was a success. With just over fifteen cases to our name, we felt we were on top. The greater Glasgow region was our domain, and several times, we spoke about extending our geographical area to cover more cases. However, like most of our 'intelligent' conversations, nothing ever came of any such proposals. It started to feel as though the other group members were getting tired of doing this. I felt stronger than ever before, and begged for more interesting cases.

This, sadly, was soon to be the end of the infamous Glasgow Ghost Hunters.

We gathered together one afternoon, in mid-September of that year, and discussed our future as the GGH. Nick was planning on moving through to Edinburgh to take up a job offer as a vehicle mechanic. John was moving in with his girlfriend and did not want to be part of 'childish' antics. Peter was relocating to Dorset, England, with his parents.

And then there was just one.

Chapter Three: Let's Get Serious

I literally lost contact with my fellow friends from GGH. I began concentrating on my career - funeral homes were never my cup of tea, to be frank. Although I enjoyed the challenges and the interaction with families, I sought a different role in my work, a job that dealt directly with people. Nursing was to become my profession.

I enrolled at my local college, and undertook a course in pre-medical sciences and anatomy. This would prepare me for my introduction to university life and academic study. I began my course in September of 1992. It was full time study, but allowed me free time in the evenings and weekends to continue my passion in the paranormal.

As I had no group left, I felt isolated. I had no one to assist me in my investigations. My contacts at the church were too busy to spend time with me. My parents couldn't care less about my interests.

As I got deeper into my college course work, I tried to focus more on my studying than on the supernatural. It was hard, in fact, almost impossible. The more I put my mind away from it, the stronger it came back at me. It felt like a 'calling'. Why me? This was not like the calling men claim to feel, when they are considering the priesthood.

Holidays I spent with the family, like most previous times. However, I felt alone. I didn't feel like myself. It was as if something was missing in my life. I couldn't point it out at the time, but it was like living on an empty stomach, churning for food, waiting to be nourished.

Many a night, I would actually cry myself to sleep. Strange? Yes. I was feeling really alone. I had lost my best friends to the big world, college and study was my focus, and my part time job in the Undertakers. How exciting!!

I awoke one morning to a new day. Somehow, I felt more alive. My mood was brighter, and I had a rush of pure energy flowing through me. I decided to get up, go out, and have a good, long walk.

I was blessed where we lived. We were just a few minutes walk from large, open woodlands. It was a grand sight on a sunny day. This morning was a sunny day. Cold, crisp, and blue sky. My walk took me around the outskirts of the woodlands. I ended my trip passing a set of small local shops. I nipped in to the newsagents to grab a soda. As I waited in the queue, my eyes caught glimpse of the Evening Times newspaper. A small article at the foot of the main spread, mentioned in bold, black lettering; "*Local Council Home, Haunted by Ghosts*"

Wow! Is this for real? I thought to myself. I picked up a copy of the print, and read it quickly before being thrown out of the shop for not paying. Sure enough, a local council flat on the other side of the city claimed to be haunted by its occupants. The journalist stated that the family were seeking help from anyone who knew about such things.

I decided to telephone the paper later that afternoon, and was transferred through to the news desk. I spoke with the journalist who wrote the piece, and offered my services. He did kind of laugh. Me? A skinny looking, 16 year old kid. What experience would I have had, at my age?

I gave him a run-down of all my investigations with GGH, and the photographic evidence from my Kodak camera. He was a bit put off by the idea, but eventually gave in, as I honestly don't think he'd had anyone else approach him offering assistance.

Arrangements were made for me to visit the family a few weeks later. I formally introduced myself, and offered to investigate their property and document any proof on camera and cassette recorder.

The first few visits were unsuccessful. No footage caught, no voices taped. Nothing. On the third and last visit I made, I decided to do my walk around whilst reciting a few prayers. I was really just acting out like a priest would do at a house blessing. I prayed what I did would get rid of any unwanted guests this family may have had. Was it fake? I don't know. I never felt anything, nor did I achieve any evidence to prove it was a real haunting.

Anyway, it was my first proper case since the split up of my team. I was now on my own, and taking on real cases. During the next few weeks I searched numerous newspapers, articles in journals, and through community posters. I was eager to search out more cases to solve. I really was becoming desperate to make a name for myself.

Reflecting back now, I know I was an immature teenage boy, aching for stardom. I was determined to make myself a name in the paranormal world. There hadn't been much on the television by the early nineties by way of paranormal programmes. Not like the vast array of shows on cable today.

My limited experience of dealing with a real haunting, especially dark forces, was going to be my true downfall by the end of that year. Catching Orb's and voices on cassette is one thing. Being physically attacked, and psychologically traumatised by an unseen, unknown force that was nothing short of pure evil was by no means what I had ever expected to face in my lifetime.

The run up to October of 1992, was easy going and fruitful. The several cases I investigated were nothing more than residual haunting. Not even a poltergeist came between my experience before and after October '92. I was about to face something; a force beyond the imagination. An entity born from the purest darkness. The extreme depths of hell.

This case was going to change, shape, and determine my very existence. My outlook in life, my career path, my family. All have been altered by the aftermath of October 8th 1992.

Chapter Four: October 4th 1992

October of 1992, I remember well. It was a bitingly cold start, brisk wind, but sunny. I was working full time at Rosedale & Son's Funeral Home, just outside the city. I was employed by this family firm, as their Junior Funeral Director, and Mortuary Assistant. It's a morbid job, I know, but I loved every minute of it. My fascination for all things scientific, stemmed from my academic studies earlier, at High school. I continued my interest in human sciences after leaving school, and graduated with further qualifications in advanced anatomy, medical virology and epidemiology, from various colleges and Universities, between 1992 and 2015. I suppose it was my wealth of higher education that led me to undertake a state registered qualification in nursing, which is what I do today.

On the 4th of October that year, I had just finished a shift at the funeral home, when I bumped into an old friend, on the street just outside the premises. It was a chap I knew who had worked for a local newspaper company as a journalist. He had resigned from the firm a few years back, but was now freelancing across the city.

We headed to a small coffee shop to grab a latte and a catch up blether. After a half hour of general chatter, he mentioned to me that a strange story had come across his desk just a few days prior to our meet. He stated that a family, living not far from the city centre, had contacted one of the major newspapers claiming to be harassed by an unseen force in their home. Ian, my journalist buddy, had decided to take on the enquiry, and made a visit to the family home.

He described to me, in fairly deep detail, what the family had been experiencing. There was banging, scratching, objects either moving on their own or being projected across rooms by invisible hands. At night, which seemed to be more active, the children had been witnessing dark figures, and mist like substances passing between walls. Faces had been appearing in mirrors, and the family dog would at times sit on its ass, front legs up, and growl at the ceiling.

I must admit, at the time I was intrigued by this story. I knew deep down I wanted this case to myself. I wanted to ask Ian if I could assist him. When was the best time, I thought to myself. Now?

"Ian. What's the chance of me helping you out with this?" I remember saying to him, as I quickly sipped on my coffee, not looking him in the eye.

I expected a laugh from him, but nothing. I peered up at him from my mug, and he was looking right at me, with a slight grin on his face. "Do you really want to help out?" he asked in return.

I set the mug down, and crossed my arms on the table. I made sure I gave him a professional stare back. "Yes. Come on man, you know me?! I've been doing house haunting for ages, and I do have experience with these things." I put my offer across and waited impatiently for an answer.

Ian sat back on the stool, mimicked me with crossing his arms, and smiled in return. "Ok. Tell you what. I'll give the family a ring, and ask them if I can bring you over this week. Introduce you to them. See what they think. Sound fair?" Ian said back.

I was overjoyed. I can still remember the excitement that grew within, as I began thinking of previous cases I had done, and the adventure this new case would bring. I nodded in agreement, and we parted ways with a handshake. Ian knew my landline number, so I didn't bother offering him it again.

The rest of that day, I waited impatiently at home, waiting for the phone to ring.

10.20pm. I was seated in my kitchen, preparing my lunch for the next day, when the wall phone jumped to life. I flew off my seat and lunged at the phone, grabbing it like a snake handler. "Hello?" I asked, trying to stabilize my balance.

"Jason. Ian here. You alright?" the voice answered.

"Yeah fine mate. What's the news?" I asked in return, not wanting any chit chat.

"It's a done deal mate. We can head over to the family house tomorrow night. You free?"

"Hell yeah! You picking me up from here?" I stretched over to my wall diary, and grabbed a pen and scrap paper. Ian gave me the time of pick up, and his number in case of delays. I thanked him and hung up. Sitting back down, I stared at the piece of scribbled paper. My mind began wandering. What was this case going to be like? Would it just be a residual haunting, or maybe even a poltergeist? I was truly excited.

October 5th.

A little after 9pm, I saw the headlights pass the dining room window. That must be Ian, I thought. I pulled on my jacket, slung my bag over my shoulder, and headed out onto the porch. It was Ian. He didn't bother coming out, just two quick flashes of his head lights, and I knew that was my call to get in.

We chatted almost non-stop on the drive over. Not just about this case, but life in general. It was a twenty-five minute journey.

Our car pulled up to a driveway, and parked behind a stationary Ford four-by-four. We both got out, and walked up the narrow, gravel path to the front door. After a few jolts at the door bell, an inside porch light came on, and a tall, dark figure appeared behind. The door opened, and we were greeted by a pleasant looking middle aged guy. Ian shook hands first, then I followed, stepping into the hallway.

"Glad you could make it this late. I work long hours in commercial driving, just got back a little after eight." The man said, ushering us into the main lounge.

Ian and I were offered a seat on the largest of the sofas. We took off our coats, and handed them to the lady, who I presumed was his wife. We sat down, almost simultaneously, and smiled at our welcoming hosts.

The tall chap was John McKinnon, aged 43, a truck driver from the north of the city. Next to him was his wife, Margaret McKinnon, 41, a school teacher in the city centre. There were three younger people, crammed together on the two piece couch.

Susan was the couple's only daughter. She was 20, and studying full time at college for a hairdressing diploma. Next to her sat Jonathon, 15, the eldest of two boys. Jonathon was in his final year at secondary school. Last, but not least, was Christopher, aged 12.

The family came across very pleasant, rather cheerful, in fact, considering what they claimed to be going through. Drinks and sticky cakes followed shortly afterwards, and we all sat having a good chat about life, jobs, the economy, and such rot. Finally, John made the move and started re-telling his family's experiences at their abode.

I had my small notebook and pen at hand, and jotted down almost everything that was mentioned. Documentation is a key tool in investigations. That's what I always tell people. Roughly forty minutes later, the description was done. Everyone in the lounge sat quietly.

"So what can you guys do to help us?" John asked, his hand patting his wife's knee.

"First of all...I am not an investigator - I'm a journalist, as you know. I'll document all findings and, if you are happy with it, maybe publish a story in one of our journals?" Ian replied smiling. "Jason here is the real deal. He's investigated many cases of house haunting, and I'm confident he will be able to help you out" Ian continued.

"Ok. So it will just be you then, Jason, that will help us get rid of whatever's in this house?" John asked, looking me right in the eyes. I sat up, tried to compose myself before answering. "Yes Mr McKinnon. I will be the investigator here. I have my own ways of finding out what's causing your problems, and hopefully banish it for good. It sounds to me, at this stage, like it's a residual problem. But then again, it could also be a poltergeist you have" I answered John's question.

"John's fine. No need for formalities here mate." He grinned back. Margaret made a snigger. "Most of the activity seems to generate late at night, not so much during the daytime. Would you be able to stay over a few nights?" again, another question.

"Yeah, that should be fine. I don't work weekends, so weekends would be much better for me." I replied.

"Ok, cool. How about coming over tomorrow night? I'm not working until the 9th, Margaret will be at home, and the kids will probably be around somewhere. It'll give you some free space to do your thing? Might as well get started soon as?" I nodded in agreement with John, and scribbled down nonsense on my notepad.

"Mum, can we go now?" a sudden voice asked. It was young Christopher, pulling at his mum's sleeve. I must admit, the three children had sat patiently for some time, without making a sound.

"Yeah on you go. Dad will be up shortly to see you." Margaret said, standing up and ushering her kids out. "Sorry about that. They're getting tired. Long day" she said, apologetically.

"That's quite alright Mrs McKinnon" Ian answered smiling. "Ok. I'll let you two have a quick talk with Jason, give him all the details you need for now. Jason, I'll see you at the car when you're ready. I need to make a few phone calls." Ian said, standing up and straightening his waistcoat. Margaret spotted the cue, and made for the coats hanging in the hallway door.

John walked Ian to the front door, shook hands and closed it after him. I was still seated, and drank the last dregs of caffeine from my cup. John came back in, and both he and his wife sat down.

"Your kind of young to be doing this?" asked Margaret, with a confused smile on her petite face.

"I'll be seventeen at the end of the month" I replied.

"A bit younger than Susan then" John butted in. "So how many houses have you been to, that've been haunted by ghosts and whatnot?"

"Quite a few actually. I've been doing this in my spare time for several years now. I feel I have enough experience to deal with a case like yours" I replied, hoping my answer was justifiable and accepted.

The married couple looked at one another, nodded, smiled, and turned their attention back to me.

"No, that's fine. Ian said you don't drive? If you want, I can pick you up tomorrow evening and bring you over?" John offered politely.

"That would be nice, thanks." I replied with gratitude.

"Ok. I don't think we can really do much tonight, not at this hour. We'll leave it 'til tomorrow. Sound okay, Jason?" John questioned

"Not a problem, cheers" I noticed Margaret standing up from the sofa. It was my turn to get my ass off the couch and bugger off out. People need their sleep!!

We said our goodbyes, and I waved at the couple as I headed back down the crunchy pathway leading to Ian's parked motor. I got in and sat down. Ian smiled, but was deep in conversation with someone on his mobile.

Shortly afterwards we stopped at my close. I said goodnight, and waved Ian off. I ran up the close stairs to my front door. Once inside I went straight to my room. I had a lot to think about - Ian was passing the buck onto me. Me? I was solely responsible now, for everything that would happen from this night onward. I never took much heed in the thought, as I was too excited about it all.

I fell asleep fairly quickly. My mind was running overtime.

Chapter Five: The First Visit.

Oct 6th

I awoke to a fine, bright, sunny morning. I actually felt good. I slept reasonably well, considering the thoughts that had been racing through my mind. I sat at the edge of my bed, tugging on my trainers. I glanced about, taking note of the state of my bedroom. It was rather messy. Books, magazines, VHS tapes, all scattered across the floor. My computer was still on, and paused at the end of the third level of Street Fighter.

There wasn't much planned that day. I had a few errands to do for Mum, and after lunchtime I had been asked by Dad to help him clear out the garage. I knew a few mates from school would be dropping by later, to pick up the games they had lent me. Maybe I would hang out with them for a few hours?

The day went by fairly uneventfully. I got through my parents rounds, saw my mates, and was finally sitting at the kitchen table waiting for mums homemade Lasagne. I must admit, nothing ever matched the feeling of munching down on mums homemade delights. It was heaven!

Shortly after 7pm, I was in my room, packing a few items together to take with me to the McKinnon home. This was to be my first solo investigation. A *real* investigation. I packed my Polaroid camera, cassette recorder, notebook, pen, flash torch and battery operated temperature rod. I was ready, I thought.

The deal was that John McKinnon was going to pick me up outside my home at around 8pm. He had phoned me earlier that day to change the pick-up time. He was a hard working family man. His job kept him more at work than at home.

I slipped on my jumper and waterproof jacket and headed downstairs to the front door.

"That you Jason?" a voice bellowed from beyond.

"Yes Mum. I'm off now, I'll be back in the morning" I replied, rummaging through my pockets for my door keys.

"Be safe now" Mum answered. She was probably sitting on the lounge couch, watching her evening soaps. Unless provoked, she wouldn't bother getting up to see me out.

I left the house, locking the door behind, and walked down the few flights of stone stairs to the close door. I lived in a Victorian tenement flat. There were eight families living in one flat, two abreast, four flights. These were common in Glasgow, especially being a Victorian city. Outside the close was a small patio garden which the council wardens would keep trimmed and clean. Skipping down the three steps to the pavement, I stood and waited for John's arrival. I had forgotten to ask him what car he drove, so at this point I had no idea what to look for.

The evening sky was dark. Not pitch black, but dark. Glasgow weather is typically overcast and dull, with a low level cloud cover – the stars are rarely seen. October evenings are usually overcast, but also have the added extra of bitingly cold wind and icy rainfall. Thankfully, that evening there was no rain.

Several cars shot past me as I stood at the roadside, hands tucked deeply into my jacket pockets. Another car came towards me and flashed its main beams twice. It slowed down to a halt just in front of me, and the passenger window dropped slightly. A face leaned over from the driver's seat.

"Hey Jason, its John. Jump in" The face smiled and flipped the door lock. I climbed in, sat down and fastened the seat belt. I looked over, smiling in return.

"Thanks again for picking me up" I said gratefully, placing my rucksack on the floor between my feet.

"It's fine. You're not that far from us anyway" John replied. "Did you bring everything you need?" he asked, shifting into fourth gear.

"Yeah I think so. I imagine I'll be doing a walk around first, if that's okay with you guys?" I asked as he sped along the M74.

"You're in charge mate. This is your thing, not mine" he said, keeping his focus on the road. "Margaret and I normally head to bed around eleven. The kids are either in bed, or out staying at friends. Either way, you'll have most of the house to yourself. Just don't come poking in our room!!" John laughed, giving me a quick glance.

I felt kind of embarrassed at the comment. However, I gave a snigger in return. "I won't do that, don't worry." I promised, still feeling the redness on my cheeks. "So...what kind of things have been happening in the house? I mean, is it just at night, or do things happen during the daytime as well?" I questioned John.

"There have been a few things happen during the day. Objects being misplaced, a few mirrors have formed cracks, lights switching on and off. But generally, most of the really bad stuff happens at night, usually between midnight and four in the morning"

I could tell by John's voice that he felt a little timid, having to recall some of the events that happened at his home. He continued giving me a run-down of specific occurrences and activities, as I tried to take notes in a hurry. It's not easy trying to scribble words in almost complete darkness. I did, at one point, think to myself; 'should I get my recorder out?' but the idea soon sank like the Titanic as we suddenly came to a stop. We were there. The McKinnon home.

For the first hour or so I spent my time sitting with the McKinnon family, huddled up on the sofa with the two boys either side of me. Susan, I began to suspect, was developing a crush on me. Maybe it was age related? I don't know for sure. It's not like I actually concentrated my efforts on her. Between the boys having a pillow fight across me, Susan eagerly smiling at me, and the parents trying to talk over the noise towards me, I felt like kid again.

Finally, Margaret ordered the kids up to bed. Susan gave an angry look at her mother, whilst her father directed a "Do as your told or else..." look in return. I tried to look away and focus my attention on Coronation Street re-runs on the TV.

The heavy thuds of footsteps passed by my shoulder as Susan grunted and moaned as she left the sitting room. John laughed her off, and Margaret came back in after seeing the boys to bed. We sat in a triangle, John switching off the television.

"We'll leave you to do your thing. We're just going to head to our room early, probably read or whatever" John said, folding the TV magazine in his hands. Margaret sat opposite, and smiled at me. "Is there anything else you need, Jason, before we go?" Margaret asked me directly.

"No, I'm fine thanks. I've got everything I need here." I replied with a smile.

"I've left you some pillows and a cover, if you want to kip down at some point." John said as He stood up, stretching his arms out wide. "Help yourself to anything from the fridge if you're hungry."

"Honestly, I'm fine, thanks. This is perfect." I felt I should stand up and thank the couple properly. I shook John's hand goodnight, and gave his wife a pleasant smile. The couple left the room, closing the door over. I could hear them talking quietly as they made their way up the staircase.

Above me, I could hear footsteps running about in the room directly above. That was the kid's room. The two boys shared a bedroom, even though they each had a room to themselves. Susan's room was at the end of the landing. I sat back down on the sofa and breathed slowly. What should I do first? Maybe I should wait a while until everyone was asleep? I made that my decision, and switched on the television again, putting the volume down to a minimum. I'd wait an hour and then begin.

I must have dozed off for a short while, as I suddenly came to with the sensation of an icy cold breeze pass my face. I sat up stiffly, looked around, but saw nothing. No one was there. Just me. The room was dimly lit by a small table lamp and the glare from the TV. I got up and headed towards the window. It was closed and locked. There was no fireplace, so where did that icy gust of wind come from? I grabbed my notebook from the rucksack, and noted the time and event.

I was awake then, that's for sure! The living room was warm. Silent. I checked my watch, 11:23pm. Surely everyone must be asleep? I emptied the contents of my bag on the coffee table, separating my equipment. I loaded up the camera with a new stock of prints, and inserted a brand new cassette into the recorder. I wrote my plan down on paper. I would start with my walk around, beginning here in the sitting room.

I pressed the record button on the machine, and left it on top of the table. Carrying my Polaroid, I began walking slowly around the room. "Is there anyone here?" I asked quietly. "If there is anyone here, could you please make a noise?"

I stood next to the window, facing the main lounge area. I snapped off a few photos and pulled out the developed prints. I gave them a quick glance, but nothing unusual showed on them. "What is your name?" I held my camera up, and began shooting towards the TV and single sofa. "I am not here to hurt you, please let me know you are with me" I asked once more.

Suddenly, out of the corner of my eye, I caught sight of an Orb float quickly over the TV and directly into the sofa chair. I hit the button on the Polaroid, but I was too late. I edged closer towards the chair, and, as I got closer, I began feeling the sensation of tingling on my forearms. I looked down at my arms, and saw the hairs standing upright. A sudden chill shot through my back, and down to my hip. I felt there was something in the room with me. I shot off more snaps with the camera.

As I stood next to the sofa I leaned down and placed my left hand on the arm rest. It felt cold. Unusual to feel this, as it was a natural cotton and wool fabric. The material couldn't retain coldness? It was at this point, this very moment, that I had the most distinct feeling. A person was sitting in the chair, staring right at me. It was the feeling you get when someone stands right up in your face, nose to nose, invading your personal space. A very uneasy sensation. I backed away a few steps, but kept my stare on the chair.

"Are you in the chair?" I demanded, hands starting to sweat. There was no reply, yet I still had this very uneasy feeling that something was in the chair, and staring right at me. I stepped back again, this time shooting off numerous photos. I didn't bother looking at them, I just wanted to shoot and flee. As I stood in the centre of the lounge, camera in one hand, pen in the other, a sudden blast of freezing air passed by me, like a slap in the face. I actually lost my footing when this happened - it was that strong. I suspected that whatever it was had run past me, giving me the nod that it was there. I looked around, beads of cold sweat forming on my forehead. Visually, there was nothing in the room, other than myself. But I felt something. It was real, it was there with me. It made itself known. The problem was, I knew that whatever it was, it was not happy.

A few minutes passed, and I felt the surroundings of the room become more peaceful. As if a bright light had shone, and the darkness had lifted. I quickly gathered the photos that I had dropped at my feet, and sat down on the main couch. I flicked through the images, one after another showed nothing. The fifth image showed a white, oval shaped Orb quite clearly, even though I thought I had been too late to capture it. The seventh photograph hit me like a brick to the skull!

The image had been taken facing the direction of the TV and single sofa chair. In the photo, the outline of a figure could be seen in a seated position on the chair. It was a greyish blue colour, but definitely a figure. A male figure. Was this the ghost I had just encountered? I was scared, to be honest, but excited nevertheless. If this was an image of a real ghost, it was my first.

I just sat there, staring at the photograph. A clock began to chime in the background, and I looked up to see the hands hit midnight. I gathered up the other images, and packed them into a folder I had brought. The main photo sat on its own. I began to think of my next step. Where should I go now? The kitchen and main hall were on this level. The staircase led up to the second floor landing, where the bedrooms and second toilet were. I decided to investigate this level first. Gathering my camera, and recorder, I got up and slowly made my way to the lounge door. I opened it gently, and exited the room.

The hallway was dark. There was a small, white beam of light coming through from the kitchen window. I could just see where I was walking and no more. I crept forward. Taking a photograph every five feet. The hallway lit up with every flash of the camera. The recorder I decided to leave on the telephone table next to the staircase. I wanted to call out again, but thought otherwise as I was scared of waking the residents up. I whispered quietly; "Is there anyone here with me? Please let me know. Show me a sign?" I asked, as I edged slowly down the hallway towards the kitchen. Nothing happened. I couldn't see or feel anything. I got to the kitchen door, which had been left ajar. I popped my head in, looked around, and decided to close it over. At the end of the hall was a storage cupboard and a small visitor's toilet. I took more shots with the camera. Eventually, I turned about and headed back down, towards the staircase.

At the foot of the staircase I quickly reviewed my photographs, which revealed nothing. I loaded the camera with more stock, and picked up the cassette recorder. I was going to venture up the stairs now.

I had literally only taken the first three steps up when I suddenly felt a push from behind. It was more like a shove, as if someone had come up from behind me and pushed me forward. It didn't feel like hands, but the force of it made me fall forward, my knees hitting the edge of the stair hard. My grip on the recorder became loose, and it fell to the floor with a thud. On my knees, I quickly looked behind me, but saw nothing. I regained my composure and got to my feet. I turned around properly, and was greeted by a hit to my left cheekbone. Something had just punched me in the face! It really did feel like a fist impacting its blow on my jaw. I fell back with the impact, my lower back coming into contact with a stair. My elbows, naturally in defence mode, took the hard fall as my body hit the deck.

I couldn't visually see anything. Even though it was dark, there was also some light coming from the outside street lamps. I was partially laying across the bottom of the stairs. My hip was aching like hell, my elbows began to burn with the carpet friction. Not only was I sweating like mad, but I also noticed my legs and hands were trembling. What the hell was this?

I had a mind to shout for help, but then what? Would I look like an idiot in front of the family? Would they think I was being pathetic? Immature? Unprofessional?

No. As much as I felt fear, I did not wish to look like a fool in front of the family. I had to regain my emotions, get back on my feet, and try reason with this force. I slowly got up, hoping to God this thing wouldn't re attack. I picked up my belongings and headed back to the sitting room.

Once I was back in the room, I turned on the overhead light. I wasn't scared of the dark, more whether this 'thing' was to return with a vengeance. At least I could see what was happening. I looked over at the clock, and the time read little past half twelve. God. Am I going to have to stay here all night, until John takes me back at eight?

I think not!

I made the unprofessional decision to leave a hand written note, saying that I had to leave for an emergency. I left the note on the coffee table, bundled all my gear into the rucksack, and headed for the front door.

The door was locked but, thankfully, the key still in. I opened the door quietly, and left. I made my way down the deserted street, until I came upon a taxi rank. Jumping in the cab, I headed back home. Back home to safety.

They always say home is a place of warmth, safety and security. Really? From what I had just experienced in that home, I could argue with that statement! Why was this force attacking me? Why was it so angry towards me? What had I done to make it so pissed off?

Then I thought, should I go back? Is there a justifiable reason for me putting my safety, and maybe even my life in harm's way? For what? To get evidence on camera, a disembodied voice on recorder? Maybe. But something in that house did not like me being there, that's for sure.

I didn't sleep the remainder of the night, as one could imagine. I closed my eyes, but just could not settle my mind from re-living the events of that evening. Although I felt safer being at home, in my own bed, I still had this feeling that I was being watched. I'm not saying I saw or felt a figure or something in my bedroom. It was just a very awkward sensation, as though a pair of eyes were staring at me the whole time.

That feeling I had experienced overnight became a reality when I finally awoke just after seven am. I sat up in bed, looked over at my computer, and saw something.

Stuck on the computer monitor was a yellow sticky note. Just like the note pads I took with me to the McKinnons home. I got out of bed, and walked over to the computer. I didn't have to peel the note off...I could read it clearly.

It was the exact same hand written note I had left on the coffee table at the McKinnon's home last night...

Chapter Six: The Investigation

Seeing that note made me think hard. What was I getting myself involved in? The thought of this case being nothing more than a residual haunting, was now far from my mind. If this entity was strong enough to knock me off my feet, and assault me physically, what else could it be capable of inflicting? My mind was running overtime as I made my way down to the kitchen to make coffee. Sitting at the table, I drank the black stuff, made notes on my pad, and began thinking of the schedule for today.

How was I going to explain this to the family? Should I say what happened to me last night, or just keep it under wraps for now?

Decisions. Anyway, I did make the plan on how to conduct the rest of the investigation. I will interview each member of the family, get their side of the story, and maybe, just maybe, something will reveal itself. That's my plan.

On that note, I got myself together. Packed my backpack with the same gear as before, and headed out. I wasn't getting a lift this morning, so I would thumb down a taxi, and make my way over.

It was a brisk cold morning with a blue sky and sun, but icy to the fingers. I had my mitts on and my woollen bonnet, the one my grandmother had knitted me for my thirteenth birthday. Today, was now October 7th. It was just after ten that morning, when my cab pulled up alongside the kerb, at the McKinnon's house. I greeted the driver and got out, stood firm, and looked out towards the large home. I smiled, but it was a smile of disagree. The home looked fantastic, just like the family houses I saw on American television series. However I knew something sinister was lurking behind those white washed doors, and grey storm shutters.

I slowly made my way up the gravel pathway towards the front door. I had just raised my first foot, when the door opened suddenly, and Christopher came running out. I almost crashed into him, if it wasn't for him swerving out my way. I saw Margaret approach.

"Sorry Jason. He's late for his football practice. Come on in" she greeted, smiling with one hand open. I smiled in return and entered, making my way to the lounge area, where John was sitting watching television. He stood up as I walked in.

"Hey buddy how's things? You left early last night?" he asked with worry.

"Yeah. I had to leave earlier than I thought, I forgot I had things to get done this morning" I answered, hoping he wouldn't ask anymore on the subject. I sat down on the sofa, placing my backpack next to me. This was the first time I really had a chance of seeing the living room properly. Considering it being a modern home, the interiors were rather retro. The lounge room, where I was seated, had seventies style wallpaper, with an equal share of picture frames and clocks that matched the time period. A lovely pine coffee table sat just beyond me, with an array of magazines spread out. The sofas were obviously bought new, but they also had that '70's' look to them. An impressive Grandfather clock stood in the far corner of the room, it's varnished oak panels, silver pendulum swinging slowly, and a moon dial in the centre piece with an eerie looking Sun that had a grim on it's face. I tried to keep my eyes from staring at it.

Margaret came in to join us, sitting herself opposite her husband. We spend the next half hour chatting about different occurrences that the family had been experiencing. The early disturbances were typical of residual haunting, but as they proceeded with their claims, the picture began to come together more clearly. Margaret had stated that a few months past, the family had taken a trip up north to the Cairngorms for a skiing trip. Whilst there, Margaret and her daughter had visited a local Orphanage, whom were having a Jumble sale. A 'Jumble' sale in Scotland, is very similar to that of a yard sale in the States.

Susan had decided to spend some of her holiday money and purchase a few objects at the sale. Teenager cosmetics and a scruffy looking teddy bear. Margaret didn't buy anything, but happily donated a few pounds towards the Orphanage funds.

"I was never too keen on that bear" Margaret butted in, as John was explaining how he sustained an ankle injury during his skiing. I looked over at her and gave her a look of question. "I mean, it was cheap and really dirty, but Susan was insistent on buying it?" Margaret continued.

"What was wrong with it?" I asked calmly, pulling out my notepad from my inner jacket pocket.

"I don't know really? I mean, I guess it was alright, it's just an old teddy, probably from one of those orphan kids. But something just didn't feel right about it" Margaret sat back on the chair, and crossed her leg, patting her skirt over. Her thick rimmed spectacles made her look like one of those high flying lawyers secretaries from the movies. For her age, I had to admit, she was very attractive. Anyway. I took down some notes, and readjusted myself on the sofa.

Come on! I was sixteen and easily excited by the sight of hot woman! Jeeze!

After being slightly interrupted, I composed myself properly and got down to serious business. I had visualized a plan in my head, and wanted to clarify with the married couple, my intentions first, before going through with it.

"Ok. My first inclination was you had a residual haunting. What that means is, you have a ghost or spirit who still resides here. They are not intelligent and wont communicate with the living. It's kind a like a tape playing then re-playing over and over. But there has been a few incidents I've witnessed since being here." My last few words tailed off and I looked down at my writing pad.

I could hear John moving in his chair. It was for a moment, quite eerily silent until John spoke.

"What do you mean, witnessed?" he asked, this time directing his stare right towards me. I fumbled around with my pen, and finally got the courage to look up.

"Last night. I was in here doing some experimenting. Nothing much, I just used my recorder and took some photos" I said back with a tremble in my tone. "Something was in this room with me. I caught it on camera. Then, when I was in your hallway, something pushed me against the stairs, and hit me in the face" I continued. I felt like a school kid in detention, shaking and scared.

John practically leaped from his chair. He stood up, looked at his wife and back at me. I felt his anger from where I sat.

"What the fuck Jason!" he snapped at me

"John." Margaret interrupted bluntly. I couldn't look at John. I peered over at Margaret, hoping to get some sympathy. She remained in her seat, but was nodding at John to sit down.

"Jason. You should have told us that instead of leaving last night. Do you not think that was important?" Margaret enquired.

"I'm sorry. It happened so quickly and I got scared. I didn't want to wake you guys" I tried offering my answer apologetically. I looked over at John to see what his response looked.

"Jason. Something like that is very important. We have three children living in this house, and it's our responsibility to keep everyone, including yourself, safe. You should have woken us and told us immediately what happened to you." John replied to my answer, but thankfully his tone was less fierce. He had sat down again, but I still felt the discomfort in the air.

"Tell us exactly what happened" Margaret asked politely.

I put my pad and pen aside, and began to recall the events from last night. The couple looked horrified after I had finished my account. I could tell they were anxious and uncomfortable with this news. John finally got up and headed towards me. He sat on a small foot stool, just in front of me, his hands clasped. He looked me in the eyes.

"Ok. I'm sorry I lost my rag with you. It just came too sudden. I thought you had been seriously injured or something" he said quietly. "We want you to stay, ok? I believe in you, and I think if we all put our faith in God, and say our prayers, this thing will leave"

I began to feel a bit more relieved at John's calmness and soft spoken words. However, I knew within me, this was not going to be that easy. I felt my attack last night was barely touching the tip of the iceberg. This entity was strong, I knew that much. I offered a nod and a smile. John leaned over and put his hand behind my head and brought me close to his face.

"I trust in you kid. If anything ever happens like that again, you better tell me first, ok? I don't want my wife or kids getting upset." His tone was bridging on whispering. I don't know if that was intentional, as to not let his wife hear. I don't know to be frank. I agreed with John with a smile.

"Come on. Lets go for a walk out in the garden, I need the fresh air." John said, getting back to his feet. Margaret had got up and left first, but headed towards the kitchen. I stood up, straightening my trousers, swiping my long, blond hair out of my eyes. John and I made our way through the hall, past the kitchen and out into the backyard. John lit his cigarette, and I stood next to him, leaning on the bin shelter. I watched him slowly drag on his puff, but I kept quiet. The breath of cold air was nice.

Following a light lunch, I sat myself back in the lounge and flipped through my notes. I decided my first approach to this case was to interview each family member individually. At least I could compare similarities and also debunk claims that seemed too far fetched. Susan would be my first interviewee. She would be home this afternoon, so I'll catch up then. The boys I would interview this evening after dinner.

Chapter Seven: The Interviews

14.45hrs. First Interview. Susan McKinnon. Location: Kitchen.

"Hey Susan. You ok letting me ask you some questions? I just need details about anything you've experienced in your home." I initiated the start of my interview session. My cassette recorder sitting upon the table, red record button depressed. My notepad and pen at the ready. Susan sat opposite me, elbows resting on the wood, holding up her bored looking expression. I know she wasn't in the mood, but I felt Susan was a key component in the activities. I needed her input badly.

With a long sigh, Susan glared over at me. I could only but smile in return.

"Well, there has been a lot of stuff going on. We've all seen shadow figures at night, especially along the main hallway upstairs, and in the lounge area. Sometimes we can hear loud banging sounds, but no idea where they are coming from" Susan stated and continued "Christopher has seen stuff in his bedroom. He says he wakes up during the night and see's a tall figure standing at the end of his bed. Probably rubbish! Knowing what he's like!"

I didn't like to speak during the taped conversation, but I felt Susan was heading off cue with her report and had to say something.

"I'll speak with Christopher anyway, get his side of the story. I just need you to give me more details on the things your saying happened" I asked, but holding a firmer tone of voice.

"Mum and dad have both seen and heard stuff around the house. Mum is always blaming me for it" Susan commented, with a slight hint of anger in her voice.

"What do you mean blaming you? For what?"

"Since I bought that teddy from the jumble sale, things have started happening. She thinks it is the bear that's causing it. Really? It's a fucking bear!!" Susan was clearly distressed over this thought and tilted back on her chair. Typical rebel teenager reaction.

"It has been known in the past for items just like bears and dolls, to be possessed by a spirit. It's this possession, is what causes activities. I'm not saying in your case it's the teddy that's the issue, but it could be a possibility" I answered with probably the most intelligent answer I could muster. I looked right at Susan, hoping to get some response from her.

"No I doubt it. It's probably the fucking house that's haunted, no the flipping bear!" she cried out with a hysterical giggle. I felt Susan wasn't taking this interview serious enough, but I had to pursue with it.

"Is there any chance I could borrow the bear to run some experiments on it?" I asked her before she decided to uplift and shoot.

"You can take it mate, I don't really like it anymore. Are you not a bit old for teddy bears?" she replied, sniggering under her breath. "I mean, your what sixteen? A grown boy?"

I started feeling a little uneasy now. I think Susan was hitting on me. I really didn't want her to see me blush or look embarrassed. How would that look?

"It's for the experiments Susan, nothing else."

Susan just sat there giving me a wide smile. At one point she even licked her lips. Oh jeeze! I tried to compose myself on the chair, flicking through my notepad. I didn't dare look up at the girl.

"Jason. You got a girlfriend?" a voice caught me off guard. I didn't look up but kept scribbling down notes.

"No Susan I don't." I answered back.

"You ever had sex?"

This question really got me angry. I stood up from where I sat, closed over my notepad and looked right at her.

"I think we will finish up here. I don't think I'll need to talk with you anymore on the subject. Thanks for your time Susan"

Susan mimicked my response, and stood up, hands pressed on the table.

"What did I say?" she asked, with a pretentious tone. "I only asked if you have had sex?"

"Susan. I'm here to try figure out what's happening in this house. I'm not here to chat up girls" my answer was blunt, I know, but she was getting on my nerves a bit.

"So I'm a girl now? Are you not into women? You gay or something?" she blurted out.

I decided not to challenge her further, and picked up my belongings and exited the kitchen. I left Susan where she stood, and didn't look back. I did feel uncomfortable. I was sexually experienced. God, I was sixteen years old, not ten! I just didn't find the talk very pleasing. I had to focus all my attention on the haunting. Something dreaded I felt, was most certainly lurking about this building, and I had to find out what.

The rest of the afternoon I spent time with the two boys. I interviewed them carefully, and noted down every detail of their experiences. There had been a great deal of similarities in their accounts, and the merging picture had began to become clearer. I wanted to talk with both parents and document their stories. I felt, as an investigator, I had to have accounts from all of the family. This would allow me to properly make a conclusion to what was happening.

18.30hrs

I was sitting alone in the lounge area, as the family had left to go get food from their local McDonald's. They had trusted me to be left on my own, without the worry of me trying to steal anything. I sat next to the coffee table, had my tape recorder out, the Polaroid charged and ready, and the teddy bear Susan had, propped up against a coffee mug.

The bear itself, didn't look very menacing. A typical brown coloured, fluffy bear with small, black beaded eyes and a green cotton pyjama set on. I actually giggled when I first saw it. This is causing all the problems? Surely not? As I rummaged in my backpack for a new pen, an icy sensation of breathing came across my neck. I sat up quickly, looking in every direction. 'what the hell was that' I thought to myself. Of course, nothing, or nobody was in the house except me. I wanted to ignore it, but the fact it was so real. It really felt like someone breathing against my bare neck, but with a heavy, cold breath.

Again, I looked down to get a better glimpse of what was inside my bag, when suddenly, I was slapped across the right side of my head. The blow knocked me off balance, and I fell over against the arm rest. This time I was scared. I repositioned myself, holding my tingling forehead and cheek with one hand. I quickly leaned across the table and hit the record button. I picked up my camera and looked around. I couldn't see anything, but nevertheless, I began shooting off picture after picture.

I got to my feet, to be able to take better shots, when again, an invisible strike impacted my right shoulder blade, sending me hurtling towards the television. I missed it by inches, and hit the carpeted floor with a thud. I drew my knees in, to attempt another stand, when, what felt like a steel toe capped boot, struck me right on the mouth and nose. I fell straight back against the floor, my head whacking the corner of the sofa. Unfortunately for me, my head hit the wooden legs of the couch, and resulted in a deep skin tear. I could feel the warmth of the blood soak into my hair. As I slowly but hesitantly sat myself up, I noticed I could taste blood in my mouth. I wiped my lips to find I had a burst lower lip. My left eye brow felt really painful to touch, and before I knew it, the eye socket began to swell over.

So here is me. Sitting on my butt, leaning against the sofa. Face swollen, lip burst, and a whopping headache coming on. I struggled to see through the affected eye, tears were nipping my eyes, and my nose was streaming. I hesitated to attempt another stand, as I couldn't face another beating. I just sat there. I looked around my surroundings, well, with what sight I had, but as usual, nothing was seen.

The clicking of the lock on the front door made me sit up straight. It must be the family returning from their dinner. What the hell are they going to think when they see me in this state? I panicked. Trying to lift my aching body up from the floor, I managed and grabbed my camera. I headed swiftly to the hallway toilet, to hide myself from the family. Once inside, I looked at myself in the mirror. Oh God, what a sight! Pulling out paper towels from the dispensary, I made a quick clean up job of my injuries. I sat down on the toilet, and noticed my hands were shaking quite badly. Am I in shock? I knew I had to make an appearance soon or the family would be worrying where I had disappeared to.

A last check in the mirror, and I exited the bathroom, closing the door quietly behind. I had just turned back around and jumped when I came face to face with Margaret. She had an expression of disbelief on her face when she saw me.

"Jesus! What happened?" she called out

"Can I speak with you and John in private?" I asked, trying my best not to look her in the eye. Margaret put her arm around me and beckoned me to follow her into the kitchen, where John was putting away groceries in the cupboards. John turned around hearing our entry. He almost lost grip of the milk when he saw the state I was in.

"What the fuck is this!?" he cried out, pushing over the stool to get to me.

"I'm sorry." I said, hands still shaking in fright. "I was in the lounge about to start my investigation with Susan's teddy, when I was attacked by something. I couldn't see anything, but it was powerful." I continued re-telling my account. "First, I was slapped, then punched on the back. I fell to the floor and then was kicked in the face. I swear it's the truth John."

Margaret still had her arm around me, hugging me closer to her chest. John approached me and placed his hand on my face, examining my wounds.

"This has to stop. Obviously whatever this thing is, it's strong, especially if it can physically attack someone." John stated, wiping smears of blood from my lip with a paper cloth. "In your opinion Jason, do you think we should move out for the time being or what?" he asked me directly. I looked at him, not smiling, more so because my face was hurting. I replied sincerely but honestly.

"No. Running away from it won't help you. We need to face it here, in the home. I will get the right things prepared so I can challenge it and force it to leave."

John exchanged looks with his wife. I could see from their expressions, they were unsure, maybe even untrusting towards me. I sensed it, and I needed to offer some form of reassurance.

"Listen. This force caught me off guard. I am normally always well prepared for these kind of attacks. I promise you I will do everything in my power to rid you of this entity. I give you my word guys." I did my best to offer the solution. Whether they took heed or not, I didn't know, I just awaited for an answer.

The three of us sat around the kitchen table. John put on fresh coffee, and Margaret attended to my wounds. I started to feel a bit embarrassed to be truthful. The couple were being so generous with me, even though I had been defeated by something unseen. How was I supposed to convince a family that I could force an entity this powerful out of their home? With what? I wasn't a priest. I couldn't perform Exorcism Rites.

Anyway. We finished our refreshments in relative silence. I agreed to stay over this night, to complete my investigations fully. I needed to do this, it sounds mad, but I felt I had to complete my initial investigation of the teddy bear and do my night time walk round. If this thing attacks again, at least I have witnesses this time. I spent the next hour or so, going through my notes, reviewing my photographs and making small talk to the parents and the two boys. We all sat mainly in the lounge, watching television. Susan was being her rebellious self, and locked herself in her room for the night.

11.20pm

The boys had been sent off to bed just before ten, and it was just myself, John and Margaret sitting up. John had fallen asleep on his recliner chair, newspaper still in his hands. Margaret was knitting but also peering up to catch what was happening on an episode of Dallas on television. I had completed writing up my notes, and packed my photos away in the backpack. I was feeling dead tired. The wounds from earlier weren't as bad now as they were at the time. Still ached though. I didn't dare fall asleep, I didn't want to look that unprofessional, even though I don't suspect either of the parents would have said anything. I had to keep myself occupied. I was still to do my night time walk round, once the parents had gone to bed.

I must have dozed off for a short while, as I remember coming to, with Pink Floyd playing on BBC One. Sitting myself upright in the sofa, and looked around me, John was snoring in the same chair, and Margaret had gone. I presumed she had either gone to the bathroom or away to bed. I stared at the TV, smiling as I watched a live performance of 'Another brick in the wall'. I was a huge fan of

Floyd and many other great bands. To tell the truth, I was a massive fan of Take That! I loved their tunes.

I took the opportunity to look about properly. The lounge was the largest room in the home. Vintage furniture, retro wallpaper, but then again, it might actually be the real deal. A sunflower clock hung just above the large mirror on the main wall. Family photo frames were dotted all over, both on the walls and perked up on shelves. Can you believe it, they also had the three duck wall ornament! For a young family, they were certainly big admirers of the cult seventies. I continued with my visual inspection when a clanging noise interrupted me. It sounded like something small had been thrown across the room.

I got up slowly, trying not to make too much noise. I searched about looking for an object out of place, when another banging sound came from behind me.

"What was that?" a voice from across the room said, startling me. It was John. The noise must have been loud enough to awaken him.

"Sounds like a marble or a stone being thrown" I replied, still standing next to the television, looking over at John. He also got up and walked over beside me. We both tried to find the location of the sounds. "The first one came from over your direction, I think? The other one was behind me, next to the window." I said quietly.

Suddenly, John cried out, almost falling into me. Something much larger had just been thrown at him, striking his back. He composed himself, and looked behind him, to see a small framed photograph laying on the floor next to him, the glass shattered into pieces. Was that what hit him? Neither of us could identify anything else. John leant down and picked up the broken fragments, placing them on the coffee table.

"I'm not happy with this" John said, his expression now looking more fearful. I tried to offer a smile, but couldn't. I also, was not feeling good. Something was most certainly amongst us.

I was just about to say something when John shouted out "Watch out!" as he pushed me to the side a large ceramic ornament which had been sitting on the third shelf of the corner cabinet, came flying through the air towards me. If John hadn't pushed me out of aim, it would have struck me bang centre in the back of my head. The object flew past my head, smashing violently against the wall. Pieces spewed all over the carpet.

"For God's sake leave us alone!!" John screamed out. We both stood our ground, watching each other's back.

Another object came flying in our direction. We couldn't see what is was, it was that quick. It hit John to the side of his shoulder and fell to the floor. A picture frame hanging above the fireplace suddenly exploded, shards of glass hurtling in all directions. The corner single sofa, where I was sitting earlier, started moving across the carpet on it's own.

"What the fuck is going on?" John growled, unable to take in what was really happening.

"It's the entity that's doing it." I replied, my eyes peeled for the next attack. We both moved over towards the window, hoping to gain some protection. I could see John was truly scared now, beads of sweat on his forehead, his hands trembling. He leaned back against the window ledge and just stared out across the lounge. My equipment was already packed in the bag, and I didn't want to move a muscle to retrieve it. Not just yet.

"What if this thing starts hurting my kids?" John enquired, still gripping the wooden ledge.

"I'll try and shout out some protective prayers, maybe they will keep it at bay for now?" I responded. I honestly had no clue if what I was about to perform would actually work. I knew around a half dozen Angel prayers off by heart, so I began my ritual by starting with the Lord's prayer and followed by Hail Mary. As I got to the end of my third prayer, I noticed the teddy bear that I had tried to investigate earlier, was sitting propped up against the television. I focused my attention on the toy as I recited the latin prayer. The bear looked as if it was beginning to move on its own accord. Even John noticed it, as he tracked my vision, and saw the bear's arms move up and down. This was a pure soft toy, no wires or mechanics, just cotton stuffing inside. The limbs could not possibly move on their own.

I moved over to my bag and pulled out the Polaroid. I handed it to John, and nodded. He began taking snaps of the bear as I completed my last recital. Once I had finished, I quickly grabbed hold of the recorder, and began taping the surroundings. I sat the recorder close to the bear. John lowered the camera after the cassette had emptied of prints. We both stared at each other then back at the toy.

"You saw that didn't you?" John asked. "I mean, that bear actually moved on its own, right?" he continued. I nodded in agreement and shut off the tape recorder.

"Yes it moved. We both witnessed it. We may even have something on camera, or on tape deck?" I answered with hope. "I have a strong feeling, that this entity has some form of attachment to the bear. Maybe it's using the toy as a vessel, somewhere to hide"

For a brief moment neither of us wanted to move an inch. Scared of something happening. Eventually, I approached the toy and picked it up. I was sure I could feel negative energy coming from it. I had a sudden wave of nausea come over me. I asked John if he could find a bag or large container. He ran out the lounge and came back in moments later, handing me a food container.

"What you doing?" he asked, passing the container over.

"If I keep the toy sealed within the container, maybe it will also keep the entity contained? It's worth a shot" I replied. The teddy was forcefully shoved inside the see through plastic box. I closed the lid over and sat it upon the coffee table.

The atmosphere in the room became lighter and more at ease. We both felt it. Deciding it was safe, John and I sat down beside each other on the couch. John stared at the box, whilst I rewound my tape recorder and began playing back. In amongst the loud hissing and crackling, I could hear a definitive voice speaking. It didn't sound like English, I had no idea what it was saying. The tone of the voice made my skin crawl. Even John looked at me as he heard the voice coming across.

"What is it?" John asked

"I don't know. It could be the entity, or another spirit trying to communicate. I'm not sure." I answered honestly. I stopped the cassette and rewound it again. We both listened in carefully and heard the eerie voice again, but still no thoughts on it's language.

"I'll leave it just now. I'm not sure what it is. I don't believe it's the same entity." I said, shutting down the machine and packing it inside the rucksack. John handed me the array of photographs he had taken. We spread them out across the glass table, and studied closely at each one. Some of the photos showed white orb's, some with fog like images. Nothing that resembled the male figure I shot previously. I still believed this force we had experienced was a powerful one, maybe even demonic.

We both agreed that remaining in the lounge was a bad idea. I couldn't have agreed more. John offered me the small room upstairs, just opposite his bedroom. It wasn't quite a guest room, but a small storage facility that John had converted into a living space. It had a fold up bed, pillows and mattress. A small bedside lamp, and that was pretty much it. It was certainly a far better and safer option than sleeping downstairs on my own.

John and I gathered my equipment, and left the lounge. Switching off the lights, we proceeded up the staircase to the rooms. A mutual decision not to carry out any further investigations until daylight. We both had injuries to heal, more so myself after my horrific ordeal a few hours earlier.

The remainder of the night was slow. I couldn't sleep much. The slightest creak or bang had my eyes wide open. Too much on my mind. I was still trying to think of the best option on how to get rid of this entity. I knew it was powerful, no question there, but how was I, a sixteen year old kid with limited experience in dealing with things this dark, going to banish a force, far more powerful than I? I had no clue. I still thought back to the toy bear. Was this entity attached to the teddy? Maybe some kind of exorcism on the bear would cleanse the home? What about taking the toy out of the house, would that stop it? I had so many questions in my head and not enough answers.

I must have finally dozed off for a while, but it was short lived as I was suddenly awoken by the sensation of someone, or something pulling at my bed covers. I actually awoke with a startle, and looked over at my watch which I had sat next to the lamp. It was little after 5am. I sat up, switched on the lamp, but nothing was there. The door was closed, although not locked, but I didn't expect anyone to come in during the night. I then noticed I had been sweating, beads of salty water streaming down my face and neck, my hair matted and twisted with dampness. The room wasn't hot, probably more cooler than normal. I didn't feel the need to get up. I just sat there, wiping the sweat with my T-shirt. I waited around ten minutes, hoping to get a sensation or feeling that something was in the room with me, but nothing. Stone dead. I left the covers off my body, as my limbs were hot to touch. My boxers were just as damp with sweat. I laid back on the mattress, turning the wet pillow over. I wasn't scared so much, just a strange feeling of being watched. Mind you, it didn't stop me from eventually drifting back to sleep.

Chapter Eight: The Attacks

The morning of October the 8th, 1992. I managed to catch up on a few extra hours sleep, following my early awakening by sheet tugging and excessive sweating. I got myself dressed, and headed out onto the main landing. I thought everyone was still sleeping, when the bathroom door opened and Susan came out, draped from head to foot in her night gown.

"Morning" she said, as she walked past me, not even giving the courtesy of eye contact. I acknowledged her greeting and headed in to the bathroom, closing and locking the door. Getting a freshen up with warm water and hot towels was a bliss. I felt human again! I was just finishing drying my sticky blond hair at the sink, when I suddenly heard a scream coming from somewhere on the landing. I quickly opened the bathroom door and looked out.

I saw Susan come running down the corridor from her room towards me. She looked terrified.

"Susan! What's wrong?" I shouted, as she ran almost into my arms. "What is it?!" I demanded, holding onto her arms. She tried to answer through muffled cries.

"I just went into my room, and shut the door, when something bit my arm" I looked at her with confusion " Look, if you don't believe me" she declared, rolling up her t-shirt sleeve. Sure enough, a large darkened purple bruise was visible, and what looked like a huge pair of teeth marks embedded in the flesh. I was taken back in shock.

"It's not just the bite marks Jason. After I felt it biting me, my bedside mirror started shaking violently. I thought it was going to shatter!" Susan remarked, caressing her arm wound.

"Ok. I don't want you going back in your room for now. I need to speak with your parents first." I said prompting her to sit down on the bathroom stool. "Stay here. I'll go get your dad."

I hesitantly left Susan sitting, and made my way down the corridor towards her parents bedroom. I stood outside and gently knocked the door. No answer. I tried again, and waited. After a few minutes, I could hear muffled voices followed by the sound of the lock being turned. A half sleeping face peered out and tried to focus on my whereabouts.

"Jason? That you?" the voice asked, coughing up a heavy chest worth of gunge.

"Yes it's me. I need to talk with you, it's very important." I replied, taking a closer step towards the grimacing face. Once John had cleared his voice and eyesight, he stared into me, and the look of worry and panic set in.

"What is it? What's happened?" he said this time more clearly and demanding.

"Susan has just been attacked. She got bit by something, and her mirror began shaking." I was about to continue, when John swung open his door fully, and brushed past me.

"Where is she? Where's my daughter?" he said sternly, storming along the corridor. He stopped suddenly, as he saw her sitting at the bathroom door. He reached down and hugged her tightly. Susan burst into tears, gripping her father for dear life.

"What happened?" he asked her, releasing his grip on her body. Susan recalled her attack in detail, as her dad listened carefully, still down on one knee. I was still standing at the doorway of his bedroom, as I felt unwanted at this moment in time. I really didn't want to interfere until John made the next move.

"Jason. We need to do something, and I mean soon. I said to you before, I didn't want this thing hurting my kids. Now look!" John stated, still angry from hearing his daughters confession. "I'm not going to let this thing hurt anyone else in this family. If I need to, I'll take them out of here until you can sort it out." He continued.

To be frank, I couldn't answer his demands. Not at that very moment. This man was furious and for good reason. He was pissed off at this force being able to physically attack his children. Bad enough that we both experienced it the night before, but not on his kids. That was the final straw for John. I knew what he was feeling, not as a father obviously, but as a mere kid myself, I sensed the father figure coming out.

John had a talk with Susan as I stood there watching in silence. Afterwards, he walked back towards me, as Susan made her way downstairs. John opened his bedroom door and walked in, waving at me to join him. Inside, I sat myself on a small chair, next to the wardrobes, whilst John got himself dressed properly. I did notice quickly upon entering, there was no sight of his wife?

"Your wife not around?" I asked him, watching as he slipped on a pair of denims. John looked round at me then back to the bedside mirror.

"She does early shifts at work. Normally leaves here around six." He answered back, making final adjustments to his belt. As a man, he was well built, and packed a good set of muscles. I dared not ask him or even make a mention of his physique, in case he thought I was weird. "I'm going to keep the kids away from here today. The boys will stay with my brother, and Susan can go visit her aunt. That way, we have time and safety to sort out this problem. I won't be here with you all the time, as I have other things to get done. Will you be ok staying here on your own?" John asked as he sat down on the edge of the bed next to me.

"I just need to get a few things from home first, then I'll come back." I replied, trying not to look him in the eye. For some strange reason I began to feel embarrassed. I felt the sensation that John had picked up on my awkwardness, and therefore stood up and backed off his distance a bit.

"That's fine mate. Once I drop the kid's off, I'll let you off at your house, but you'll need to make your own way back here. I'll give you the spare set of keys. I'll not be back for a few hours. You ok with that?" John said, slipping on a brown, checked jacket. I'd never seen one before, but I did find out much later on, it was a traditional Harris Tweed blazer. A real home- made Scottish men's wear, made in the Outer Hebrides. So Cool!

I agreed with John's plan, and proceeded to head downstairs to the kitchen, where I would see Susan somewhere about. John had told me to make myself at home. I could have cereal and toast for breakfast, or porridge if I knew how to make it! I decided on the latter, as my mother had taught me many times how to make the white gruel. 'always make yer porridge wae salt and herrings' This was my mum's way of teaching Scots recipes, always in a Glaswegian slang, that no other person on earth would understand!

Porridge with salt and what???? Yes. Bloody herrings! Those tiny wee fish that smelled like rotten socks. Supposedly, it was a Highland way of eating porridge?

Regardless of taste, I succeeded in producing a nice bowl of Quaker's Oats, not quite Scottish, but did the job nevertheless. Susan just stared in confusion as I made my miracle substance. She went with a bowl of Cornflakes and half a gallon of milk. John bypassed breakfast and went straight for the coffee maker. We three sat down together at the table, and make small talk about the day's plans. Susan was quite happy to be out of the house for the day. John went over his duties and work rota with his daughter. I pretty much sat there in quietness, slurping down my hot oats.

The two boys were still asleep upstairs whilst we ate breakfast. That was short lived, as John went hammering up the stairs and began yelling for them to get up and dressed. A short while later, the lads came down to the kitchen. They greeted me with a smile, then headed to the cupboard for their wheat cereals.

11.15am

Finishing breakfast I made my way into the lounge and sat down on an armchair next to the window. It was a bright morning, the rays of sunshine filtering through the mesh curtains. A nice cold breeze slipped through the open window. It felt good. I sat my evidence on my lap and weeded through the collection of photographs, tossing aside the ones I felt showed nothing of importance. At the end, I had only mustered a mere four decent pictures, the ones I caught the orbs, and the shots taken of the outline of the male figure. I reviewed the tape recorder for the fifth time but only static and hissing sounds resulted. Not much to prove really? The attacks and disturbances up to now, where only visual proof. I need more solid evidence.

Barely had I time to finish my thoughts, when I was startled by a sudden crashing noise centring from the kitchen area. I leaped to my feet and ran through to the scene of the noise. Pushing open the wooden door to the kitchen, I was confronted by a complete mess. The centre table had split in two, both ends facing inwards. Shattered crockery and glass tumblers, layered the vinyl floor. The two shaken boys stood beside each other at the corner of the room next to the back door. The fear on their faces and the trembling of their bodies, was enough to ensure something terrible had just occurred. I swiftly ran over to them and held them together. Christopher began weeping in my arm. He looked up at me, tears and nasal deposits ran down his pale face.

"What happened?" I asked him, attempting to wipe his face with my sleeve. He coughed and sniffed before answering.

"We were sitting at the table, and then a loud banging noise made us jump. We both stood up and that's when the table broke into bits." Christopher remarked sobbing. "We stood back from it and that's when stuff starting flying in the air" he continued his story.

"What do you mean stuff? Flying?" I asked cautiously.

"Yeah, bowls and glass tumblers came flying out of the cupboards and smashed everywhere. One even hit him" Christopher stated, pointing at his brother. I looked over at Jonathon and clearly saw a cut embedded in his left arm. It was bleeding, but not too bad. I stepped between the boys and took a long roll of paper towel from the dispensary, handed it to Jonathon and let him wrap it around his injury.

"Ok guys, we better leave here now. Do you want to head into the lounge just now?" I said, ushering the lads out of the war zone, making sure to skip over the shards of broken glass and ceramics.

The three of us made our journey to the safety of the lounge. Once inside, the boys sat down on the larger of the two sofas. I stood guard at the door and awaited the presence of their dad. What the hell was I going to tell him? He'll go mental!

Sure enough. A few moments later, I heard footsteps come thundering down the staircase and away towards the kitchen. Shouting and swearing was heard by all three of us. Jonathon actually sniggered at hearing his dad curse in tongue. Although barely older than him, I still felt the adult in this situation.

"Better not let him see you laughing mate. I reckon he's going to be well pissed off." I remarked, giving the teenager a growl. Christopher sat in silence, rubbing his nose with his sweater sleeve.

John came bursting in, and saw the three of us. He ignored me for a second and stared at his sons.

"What the fuck??" he growled, standing strong, hands on the hips. I felt like interfering, but decided to stay put for the time being.

"It wasn't us dad." Jonathon said, his grin quickly vanishing into a state of panic. Christopher began crying again.

"Jason?" John asked, now looking in my direction. I didn't have time to make up a story, it just came out in bursts.

"I was in here when I heard a loud crash. I ran into the kitchen and saw your boys standing together. The table had been smashed up and objects thrown around. It wasn't them. You know what it was." I made my stand and offered a true account of what the boys had disclosed.

John's stare didn't move. He eyed me up and down, maybe looking for signs of false testimony. Finally, he looked back towards his children, his facial expression now becoming more relaxed and warmer.

"Ok, I believe you. I want you both to get your jackets and meet me back here in five minutes. Go!" John demanded. The boys didn't need a second warning, they got to their toes and sprinted out of the lounge. Their stamping feet running upstairs.

John approached me slowly, wiping the beads of sweat from his brow. I could see he was angry but also worried. I didn't say anything. I waited for him to start talking.

John sat down on the armchair, and held his head in his hands. He stared at the floor nodding in disbelief. He murmured words under his breath, then looked up.

"Jason. You need to do something. I can't have this thing harming my family anymore. I've had enough already." He gave me that sympathetic look, but I think it was a look of need. I knew I had to say something that resembled an answer to his question. I wasn't even sure what I said next would comfort him.

"I'll do what I can to get rid of it John." I made my mark and I knew John would hold me to it. "I'll get the few things I need from home and come back later this evening."

John nodded in agreement and stood up next to me.

"Are you sure you can get rid of it? I don't want it in my house." John said, placing one hand on my shoulder.

"Yes I'm sure." I lied, giving him a false smile. It was the best I could do under pressure.

"I'm taking the children away tonight. I'll be back with Margaret. I'll drop you off at home but you'll need to make your way back." He continued.

"Yeah, you told me that earlier." I answered with a smile. John smiled back, and actually giggled.

"Oh sorry. I forgot." He took his hand away, and moved over towards the doorway. He shouted out for the boys to hurry. I decided to utilize this moment and gather all my belongings. I had the feeling we were about to leave promptly.

The front door opened and John led the way out, the boys quickly heading out first, and down the gravel pathway. I followed en suite, and turned round to see John locking the door, shoving the keys inside his denim jacket. He followed behind and pointed at his car. Jonathon and Christopher were already standing at the rear doors waiting for the car lock to open. I stood at the passenger door and looked back at the house. It didn't have that wonder feeling it had a few days earlier. Something foreboding had taken hold of it. It was as if something was looking back at me. Something uneasy...something evil?

I was dropped off at the foot of my street. John gave me a quick goodbye and yet another reminder to make my way back to his home by around nine that evening. The boys gave a slight wave as the car sped off. I watched in silence as the car turned the corner at the end of the street and vanished. I turned around and made my way up the three steps to the close door. I had a security key that allowed me access into the tenement. Once inside, I slowly began climbing the stone stairs to my landing. The weekly washman must have been as I could smell the distinct aroma of damp mops and bleach.

I entered my flat, closing the door behind. I shouted out to see if any of my parents were at home, but no answer. I suspected at this time of day that they were both still at work. I headed into the kitchen and made a fresh pot of coffee. Sitting down on the corner stool, I opened my rucksack and emptied the contents onto the kitchen worktop.

'None of this means anything.' I thought, flipping through the photographs once again. There wasn't much evidence and that was fact. Everything that had occurred recently was simply visual, and word of mouth. How was I going to document such a case without real evidence? The coffee pot beeped, alerting me to it's completion. I poured a hefty mug full, dropped about five spoonfuls of sugar and topped it up with milk.

I had to get proper equipment for tonight. A Roman Missal, a crucifix, holy water and a blessing from Father Michael O'Brannon, my local parish priest. Father O'Brannon knew me well. I had been a part of the church choir and the Rosary group, as well as the Youth club on a Wednesday evening. He knew I was interested in ghosts and hauntings, although a skeptic at the best of times, did offer me the odd prayer of protection every time I went on an investigation. However. This case was slightly different from all the others I had been to. This case was real.

I finished my refreshment and headed up to my bedroom. I gathered some fresh clothes for this evening and decided to take my small, black hand case. It was small enough to put the essentials inside. I didn't want to carry the recorder or camera with me this time. I made the decision to telephone the church and speak with Father O'Brannon. I gave him a brief run down over the phone, as to what I had experienced at the McKinnon's house. He clearly came across rather angry. He tried to persuade me from taking this any further, but I assured him I was ready to deal with it. After a long forty five minutes debate, I agreed with the young priest, to drop by the Sacristy and pick up some items he stated he wanted me to take.

That done and dusted, I laid across my bed and began thinking. Well, the thinking must have been hard going, as I fell asleep pretty quickly.

The sound of the door bell ringing awoke me with a scare. I sat up like a shot, still on top of my bed. My t-shirt soaked in sweat. Oh God, I smelled terribly! I swung my legs round and got to my feet. Skipping down the small flight of carpeted stairs, I approached my front door. I could see the red shape behind the small round glass port hole. It was the postman. I opened the door, greeted him with a smile, took the collection of envelopes and closed over the thin pine door. I didn't want the guy taking a sniff of my body odour. How shameful would that be! I didn't bother looking at the mail, it was mainly all for my dad anyway. Bills, payment letters, debts, lawyers, the usual shit. I dropped the bundle onto the hallway table, and made my way for a quick shower.

5.25pm

Mum and Dad would be home by around six, so I didn't want to be here when they got home, in case I got the third degree regarding my night's adventure. I got dressed, double checked I had everything I needed, and left the flat.

Outside, it was already dark. Cold air with an icy breeze. I had my Parker jacket on, woollen scarf and beanie, and my favourite mittens. I crept along the pavement, heading south towards the church. The pavement was icy as hell, and I feared I would slip and break my leg! I loved the winter but not the icy roads.

Just under fifteen minutes later, I approached the front doors of St Michael's . They were tall, heavy oaked doors, with a brass handle, which of course, was freezing to touch. I opened the doors and slipped in quietly. I couldn't remember if there was Mass on at this time, or if one of the evening groups were in action. I walked down the side aisle, taking in the beauty of the Stations of the Cross paintings. At the end of the aisle sat an impressive statue of our Lord, holding two children in his arms. An iron candle holder in front with a half dozen or so, burning red candles. I knelt down on the stool, crossed myself, and asked Our Lord for protection. I had my eyes closed as I repeated my request, when a hand suddenly touched my head. I looked up from my kneeling position, and saw Father O'Brannon looking down on me.

"Evening Jason" he said with a calmness in his voice. I smiled at him and got to my feet.

"Hi Father. Thanks for letting me see you." I answered.

"Come with me. Father Johnston is using the Sacristy just now for a meeting. We can use my office." The priest led me through a few narrow corridors, and into a small, square office. It was like a typical office you would find, files, archives, cabinets, typewriter. He sat down and offered me the spare chair.

"So what is it your up against? You said it was a malevolent entity?" he began his questioning, taking notes on a small pad.

"Yes. It is indeed active and quite violent. It attacked all three of the kids. I saw most of it. The parents just want rid of it." I began.

"Ok. First thing you need to know, is protecting your own safety. Your life comes before anyone else." When Father O'Brannon said this, I felt slightly annoyed. If I am putting my life in the way of protecting another, would God not see that as being a saviour? I wanted to challenge him on my thought, but just left it aside.

"Our Lord Jesus will be there to watch over and protect you always. Never forget that. Use this crucifix as a means of pushing any dark force back to where it came. If this entity was to reveal itself, do not hesitate to use the holy, blessed water."

I nodded as the priest went through the ritual in detail. He held open the Roman Missal, and placed several bits of paper between the pages.

"I have chosen certain prayers for you to use. I've page marked them with slips. Follow my instructions carefully. I've written them on the inside of the Missal. If in doubt, just turn and leave." He stated with firmness, whilst handing me the book. I took the objects and placed them carefully inside the black hand case.

"Thanks Father. I hope things won't go as far as this. Maybe a few simple prayers will make it leave?" I said in return, thinking I would get a positive answer from the clergyman.

I got up, shook the priest's hand, and made my way out of his office. As I walked back down the aisle towards the exit, I looked around the magnificent church, and admired the pure holiness of my surroundings. It gave me a sense of power. A sense that nothing could harm me.

Leaving the church, I stood outside, back into the cold and darkness. I wrapped my scarf tighter around my neck. It was still too early to head over to the McKinnon's, so I decided I would stop by the library for a last check on my plans. At least the library was open until eight.

7.50pm

I made the decision to walk it to the home. It took me just over forty minutes. At last, I stood at the front lawn. I looked directly at the house. It was menacing. Dark windows, pale grey wooden frontage. The trees in the garden blew fiercely. I suddenly had the most uneasy feeling of dread and panic. What the hell was I doing here? I had to go through with it. Not for me, but for the family. I just hoped someone was in, even though I had the spare set of keys, I now felt extremely worried about entering the house on my own.

Chapter Nine: The Confrontation

I rang the door bell and waited. Nothing. Again, I pressed the plastic key several times, stood back and waited, tucking my hands inside my jacket pockets. The wind blew angrily, the icy temperature biting at the face and ears. I treaded my steps just to keep my feet from freezing over.

This was the one thing I didn't want. To be inside the house on my own, but here I was standing out in the cold, on my own, holding a set of keys to the damn place. I hated my decision, but I knew I had to go inside.

I inserted the brass key into the lock and jiggled it around until I heard the latch click. I slowly pushed open the door, and was greeted with an even colder blast of air. I stepped in and closed over the door. It was dark except from a small table lamp, glowing with a warm yellow ambience. It made me smile. I walked down the main hall and popped my head into the lounge. It was almost as dark, but an outside street lamp shone it's beam through the netted curtains, so I could barely make out the confines of the room.

The house was unusually cold, even for this time of year. Most families would have their heating on all the time? Some reason, this family decided not to keep it on, hence the freezing temperatures. At least I was well wrapped up. I proceeded down the corridor to check out the kitchen and lower level bathroom. Everything seemed ok. Well, except the kitchen. The debris from this morning's poltergeist attack was still evident. It shot a chill down my back just looking at the state of the area. The small bathroom was empty. My initial conclusion at this stage was that the lower ground floor of the house was clear.

What a relief! I thought. If anything is going to kick off it's going to be upstairs. That's where the last attack came from. I hoped Susan was alright after her encounter in her room? Maybe this entity is still lurking in there? Or maybe it's moved on to somewhere else within the home. I had to do my proper checks.

Each room had to be visually checked for signs of activity. In other words, objects and furniture having been moved or misplaced. Looking for signs of broken or cracked glass, mirrors and crystal ornaments. In some cases, there has been reports of unseen hands writing messages on walls and ceilings. Again, part of my investigation. So far, nothing showed up. I continued my walk round, finishing at the foot of the stairs. This was the part that got my nerves up. The physical attack I got in this particular part of the house, was still very clear and painful to remember.

It was time to arm myself. I had no idea what laid beyond the top of the stairs? I stood there quietly, holding onto the banister and reaching into my hand case, I withdrew the wooden crucifix and Missal. The plastic bottle of blessed water was in my inner pocket of the jacket.

I was ready...I thought. I began to recall the words Father O'Brannon had said earlier, about being strong and think positive. Our Lord was with me. The thoughts began to give me inspiration and faith. I smiled again, but to myself this time, as I started my slow trek upstairs. Each stair had a creaking sound, as if it were moaning in hurt.

I stopped half way. My hand still holding the rail, I looked up towards the top landing. I was sure my eye caught a glimpse of a dark shadow fleeting past. Was it just my eyes or did I really catch something? My heart rate was gradually increasing to the point I felt palpitations. Sweat began to form on my brow, even though it was cold as hell.

What the heck is this now? I thought aloud. I swear music was playing. It was coming from beyond the top landing, maybe somewhere around Susan or John's bedrooms? To make it even more freakier, it was a hymn I knew ' *Nearer, My God, to Thee'* Of all things, why would it be a church song? Is that not kind of taking the piss? I pushed on, each step I took was one step closer to facing the truth. The music still played in the distance, but as I reached the final step, and placed both feet firmly on the carpet, the music seemed to vanish.

A sudden blast of cold air rushed past me, as if something had ran along the corridor. I looked in both directions but didn't see anything. My grip on the crucifix was even tighter now. My fingers were damp with sweat. Even as the house felt cold, I was burning up inside.

A door opened. I quickly tried to focus my sight on it's whereabouts. I think it came from the last room on the left. The bathroom. I flicked on the landing light, and was welcomed by a warmth atmosphere as the corridor lit up in amber. I began walking towards the bathroom, slowly pushing open each room door as I went.

Out of nowhere, I felt an almighty shove from behind. I went flying forward, the crucifix and book dislodging from my hold and we went in different directions. I landed hard on the floor, my head taking the impact.

'Come with me'

As I laid across the carpet, my forehead bleeding, a distinct and loud disembodied voice shouted out. Come with me? Am I sure that's what I just heard? I pulled my knees in, and pushed myself up with my hands. I swayed slightly as I fought to gain my balance. I couldn't see where the objects had landed. I looked around to see if anything had fallen behind me, when I was suddenly grabbed, by what felt like a very strong pair of hands. The spectral fingers clasped their grip around my throat and tightened.

My body felt lifeless as I was picked up about five inches from the floor, both my hands at my neck, trying to pull away the unseen hands. I wheezed and gagged, tears streaming down my face. I knew I was suffocating. I cried as I tried to breath gulps of air. Then, just as violently and quickly, my body was thrown to the side, like an unwanted ragdoll. I struck a small panel table that sat just outside Susan's bedroom. It smashed with the impact of my weight, shards of splintered wood projecting through the air.

My God, the pain....

I was too scared to attempt another stand, so I laid there, mixed in amongst the broken panels, large gashes to my upper torso and arms, blood seeping through my clothing. The jacket I had worn was flimsy. It didn't take much to tear it open. My shirt was a mess. It had been pale blue when I put it on earlier, it was more crimson now! The deep cut to my forehead must have been worse than I imagined. The blood flow wasn't stopping.

I wrestled myself out of the carnage and sat up on my butt. As usual, there was nothing to be seen. Another door slammed, but I had no clue to it's whereabouts. Gaining a little more strength, I clambered to my feet, brushing off fragments of wood from my chest. I pressed my hand against my forehead, trying to put pressure on the wound. Looking about I caught glimpse of the crucifix, laying on the carpet not far away. Hesitantly edging forward, I bent down and picked it up, grasping it tightly in my hand. I said a quick prayer in my head and asked for help from my Guardian Angel.

The Missal was also on the floor, but over near by the spare bedroom door. It rested against the skirting board, pages torn out and littered across the area. I headed straight for it, and once I retrieved the book, I sat down on a small chair that was seated just outside the parents room. My whole body ached. The bleeding had finally subsided, but that didn't help the fact I had just been brutally attacked by something I couldn't even see!

I flipped through the ripped pages of the book, nodding in disbelief. What form of entity can be that malevolent to destroy a holy missal? In fact, thinking about it, a normal spirit wouldn't have the energy to physically attack someone. Was this demonic? I drew conclusions to this thought and withdrew my small note pad from the inner jacket pocket. I had a section numbered on demons and demonology. Maybe what I'm dealing with here, I may have documentation on it. I swiftly searched through the labelled pages until I suddenly stopped at a page. *'Demonic forces and style of attacks'*

As I sat thumbing my way through the pages in detail, I also felt the surrounding air drop in temperature. It was beginning to get very cold again, the same sensation I felt at the top of the landing. Was this thing returning?

Finishing reading, a slipped the pad away and stood up. Looking in every direction I decided to make my way towards Susan's room. If this entity was indeed demonic, it would soon show itself again, I just prayed for my sake it wouldn't be fatal. Approaching the room door, I stopped, placed my hand on the brass knob, slowly turned it and pushed open the door. Inside there was nothing. Nothing out of the ordinary that is. I entered slowly and stood next to the bed. There was a small bedside lamp on which was enough to light the room up.

"I know you can hear me. Tell me why you are here?" I called out, my eyes scanning the room for a response. "Why are you hurting this family?" continuing my verse. There was no response, just silence, except from the humming in the distance from the radiators.

"I am asking you to please leave. This family don't want you here anymore!" this time my approach being more forceful. A sudden foul odour came over me, and I knew it wasn't me. It smelled like a cat or a dog that had been rotting for weeks, it was terrible. The stench finally became almost unbearable. My hand across my nose, I began moving out of the area and towards the door. A crashing sound came from behind me, I turned to look back and saw the clothes cupboard in pieces across the floor. Something powerful had just pushed it over.

'Get out!'

A voice screamed out. It was distinctively male and frightening, a disembodied tongue that shot fear straight at me. I quickly exited the room and ran halfway down the corridor, before coming to a sudden halt. At the far end of the landing, I noticed the outline of a tall, black shadow, it's form resembling that of a huge man, it's silhouette clear against the backdrop of the white netted curtains. It just stood there, never moved an inch. Likewise, I couldn't move a muscle, more in a state of fear than shock. Was this the demonic entity I had been hearing and feeling?

I quickly made the decision to turn around and head towards the parent's room. Maybe in there, I would find some protection? I had no clue what I was doing. I followed through with my thought and proceeded to make my way back down the landing and into John and Margaret's bedroom.

Inside, I was greeted with a feeling of warmth and security. Lamps on either side of the double bed were switched on, giving the room an ambience of safety. I closed the door and sat on a small foot stool, just behind the door. My heart rate was up, palpitations were racing, and cold sweat forming over every part of my body. Even my hands were trembling.

Taking my notebook out, I found the section on Angelic protection. There was about half a dozen or more, assorted prayers and incantations I could use for my personal safety. Saint Michael had always been my favourite archangel, and was actually my communion name. I decided to read over St Michael's prayers as well as St Raphael and the Rite of Exorcism as laid down by the Vatican II. Although I couldn't technically carry out an exorcism, as I clearly wasn't an ordained priest, I had been told, in the worst case scenarios, I could use certain phrases from the Rites, which would hopefully be enough to banish whatever being I was fighting. Really? Well, that's what I was told by a retired clergyman. I suppose it couldn't do me any harm?

Chapter Ten: Deliver me from evil

Gathering my energy and stamina, I got to my feet and took a few steps closer to the side of the bed. Across from me was a bedside table and a pine bureau which had a variety of cosmetic artefacts displayed including a vintage mirror stand. That I suspected, was Margaret's table top for donning her makeup and what not. At the far end of the room from where I stood, was the bedroom window.

I opened my notebook and flipped over the bookmark. Coughing once then swiping my hair back, I began reciting my first series of prayers.

"Sancte Michael Archangele, defende nos in proelio, contra nequitiam et insidias diabolic esto praesidium. Imperet illi Deus, supplices deprecamur, tuque, princeps militia...."

My prayer for protection by St Michael in Latin, was quickly interrupted by a sudden vibration emanating from the pine bureau. I glanced over to see a small, hand held mirror begin to shake on it's own accord. Then, I witnessed the other objects on the table begin to violently move around. I actually believe the entire bureau had begun to vibrate from some unknown force.

"...oh prince of the heavenly host, by the power of God, thrust into hell, Satan and all evil spirits who wander through the world for the ruin of souls. Amen"

I completed my prayer, but by this time, not only was the bureau shaking, the double bed was now moving across the vinyl floor towards me. I jumped out of harm's way, as the corner of the bed struck the door, barricading me in. Something whistled by, and exploded against the wall behind me. Objects were now being projected at me.

"Exsurgat Deus et dissipentur inimici ejus et fugiant qui oderunt eum a facie ejus"

I began to recite the first phase of the Exorcism rite as written in the Vatican manual for Diocese Priests. It was given to me by my grandmother, whom had obtained it decades earlier from a good friend and retired Catholic minister. The book had been well used and aged, but I was able to dictate enough scripture from it before it was unreadable. Whether these prayers would help I don't know. It was worth trying.

As I continued my unauthorised exorcism, the room began to feel very oppressive and heavy. The air it'self, became dry and hard to breath. The temperature had dropped considerably, and I was able to see my own breath. My skin felt very unusual. I looked down at my hands and arms, and my skin appeared to be greyish and shiny. Tremendous pains shot down my spine to my legs, and at one moment, I lost my balance and fell back against a pile of plastic boxes.

"Behold the cross of the Lord, flee away ye hostile forces. May the mercy of the Lord be upon us, Lord hear my prayer. Cast ye out, unclean spirit, and every Satanic power and adversary, every legion and every diabolical sect, follow thy light into the kingdom of heaven."

Speaking out the last of the ritual prayer, I was not confronted by happiness or peace, but with an unspeakable force of energy that took me from my feet, sending me airborne across the top of the bed, crash landing on top of the bedside cabinet, the lamp disintegrating under my stomach, white cords of wire entangling my neck and arm as I slumped to the side of the mangled table.

In the midst of the violence and the growing sounds of objects being thrown about, I caught the sound of the bedroom door, attempting to be opened. Although my sight was hazy, and I could feel the warmth of blood from my ear drum, I tried sitting up.

"Jason!" a voice shouted from beyond. "Open the door!" it called out again. It was John.

I looked across the room from where I was laying, and could see the door being pushed or kicked from the outside. John was trying his best to get inside. I also heard the faint whimpering voice of Margaret.

"I can't...move..." I tried calling back, but my voice was drowned out by the activity within the room. It's hard to believe, but the noise inside the bedroom was that loud, you had to shout above and over it to be heard. Tables were either vibrating hard, personal items being thrown about, picture frames on the walls had been imploded or forcefully pulled off, and the double bed was still shaking on it's four wooden posts.

John had managed to pry the door open just enough to peek inside. I saw his partial face peer in and his expression of complete shock at the sight unfolding.

"Jason. Can you hear me?" he yelled out, catching sight of me slumped at the side of his cabinet.

I shouted in response, hoping he would hear my words over the deafening environment. He did, with an acknowledgment of a nod.

"I can't get in. Stay put, I'm going to get help" John responded eagerly. He slipped his hand through the opening of the door and gave me a thumbs up.

I raised my bloody hand to offer him a wave, but even doing this basic task was an effort. My arms ached terribly, the pain in my back was unbearable. I hoped to God I hadn't damaged anything serious, I couldn't face the thought of being paralysed. The door closed over, and I was left alone, again.

The noise within the room was peaking to a point of ear ache. It looked as though someone had came in and totally trashed the room, smashing up everything and anything. I managed to haul myself back on my feet. I picked up my crucifix and bottle of holy water, and stood tall. I was going to try and fight this demon. For the sake of myself and the family. No one should be allowed to suffer under the influence of something this evil. I had to do it.

I was scared to death! Understandable. Here I was, standing in the centre of complete chaos, facing a powerful force which I believed to be demonic. Head to feet in torn, bloodied clothing, a kid with a crucifix and holy water.

I knew in the darkest regions of my mind, that this could end badly for me, even fatal, but I felt the empowerment to do something right. Maybe God would intervene and save me, who knows?

I made my last effort of a challenge to this being, spouting out more Latin prayers and protection spells on myself. I raised the crucifix to eye level and spun round in a complete circle, reciting a prayer to each corner of the room. When I ended up facing the window again, just opposite from where I stood, a smell of metallic burning arose from nowhere. It was strong, even overpowering, burning the insides of my nostrils. As I looked around me for explanations to the supernatural occurrence, my eye caught something.

From next to the window, rising up from behind a cabinet, a black fog began to manifest. It rose up slowly at first, then it began to form shape. The shape of a tall, black, menacing figure. It must have been at least seven foot in height, its shoulders and head clearly outlined, and then from within the black shape of its head, a pair of small, oval shaped slits formed, with piercing red eyes, stared right at me.

I could feel it drawing me towards it. It felt like a magnet, even though I couldn't move physically, my insides were being drawn closer to the entity. I think it was my soul being taken. I remained standing where I was, but I was unable to flinch an inch. I could feel myself become drained of energy, feeling of light headedness, and my limbs became weak. This demonic force was killing me, taking every ounce of my life force away. If this continued, I was sure to be dead soon. Then what? It would do the same thing to John and his family.

No way! I couldn't let this happen.

Within my quickly deteriorating body, I said a final prayer to Saint Michael, confessing my sins and asking for forgiveness. As I continued my prayer in my head, the dark figure seemed to grow stronger. Its shape became more defined, its colour a striking jet black. It was developing stronger as it fed off my soul and spirit.

I eventually dropped to my knees, losing grip on the crucifix. The plastic bottle rolled out my hand and across the floor. I knew my end was close, I could feel it.

As I knelt in defeat, awaiting my fatal end, a very bright white beam of light came radiating through the bedroom window. It shone so bright I had to close my eyes. The most ear piercing scream shattered the noise within the room, silencing everything else.

I braved my luck and opened one eye, and tried to focus on the light. The dark figure was diminishing within the beam, as if the light was enveloping itself around the entity, consuming it whole. I caught for only a brief second, what looked like a hand, within the circle of white light, moving around. Then, another hand and a lock of grey hair, followed by what looked like white satin cloth. What was it?

An angel?

I never saw it again, it was literally over with in a matter of seconds. The demonic entity within had almost vanished from sight, and only this ball of bright light remained. It seemed to hover a few feet from the ground, and had this humming sound emanating from it. The other noise from the room had also gone, and it was now almost silent, except from this humming.

Although still remaining lethargic and on my knees, I raised one arm out towards the ball and I began crying. I wasn't sure what or who it was, but I knew one thing for certain. It banished the demonic creature to somewhere I hopefully will never see.

The ball of light began to dull in brightness, and shrink in size, to a point where it was about the size of my fist. It hovered a few feet from me, before disappearing in a click. I bowed my bleeding head and thanked God for protecting me. Just as I did, a sudden bang brought me around.

I looked behind me and saw a pair of feet kick through the bedroom door. A few seconds later, I saw John and another guy force their way in. Margaret followed en suite.

"Jason you alright son?" John asked, scooping me in his arms. I couldn't help it, I burst into tears and wept in this strangers arms.

Margaret took over, and helped me to my feet. John and his friend surveyed the room and were clearly taken back by the carnage that had occurred.

In the hallway, I sat with Margaret and John, and began to re tell my event. They listened carefully but at times, with expressions of hatred and anger. After what felt like hours, my story had came to an end.

The demonic entity had been challenged, maybe not successfully by me, but something higher than me, something godly, had intervened and delivered me from evil.

By the time midnight had came, I was in hospital, being treated by emergency physicians, attending the horrific wounds inflicted upon me by the demonic force. The doctors were shocked at the degree of savagery, and the seriousness of the injuries, they were amazed I hadn't died from severe blood loss.

As you can imagine, my parents soon found out what had happened to me, and although sceptical about my attacker being a demon, they suspected more a 'human' was at blame. Nevertheless, a police enquiry was initiated, and a full investigation underwent. This last nearly a month until the final conclusion resulted in "injuries sustained by unknown attacker"

What can I say...what could I say? Only myself, John and his family really knew what happened in their house. Only myself came face to face with pure evil and almost died. The event of October 8th, 1992, never left me.

For just over two years following the incident, I was under the care and treatment of a Consultant Physician, receiving medical treatment for anxiety, depression, nightmares, and pain management for my injuries. It was almost three years before I felt strong enough to undertake paid employment again.

In the summer of 1995, I was in Glasgow city town centre, having a coffee with a close friend from work, when the discussion of demonic haunting came about. We spoke and debated over the subject for quite some time. It was later that evening, back at home, I was still pondering over our earlier discussions, when a question kept popping up in my head.

'If I went through that ordeal, what do other people go through, especially families and those with no experience of this type of phenomena?' It got me thinking serious.

I was soon to be starting on a quest, a life's journey of study and practice in the art of Demonology. By the end of 1995, I was enrolled on an academic course on the subject, run by the Jesuit Priests in Rome, Italy. The year after, my studies progressed and I completed an eighteen month training course on Biblical and Modern Demonology at a University in Paris, France. My practical experiences begun the following year, when I began advertising myself locally at first, then nationally, as a specialist in violent house haunting.

Today, at the grand old age of 40! I have been working as a Demonologist and expert in violent haunting cases for over 20 years. I am acknowledged as a world renowned demonologist, lecturer and investigator. My experiences and knowledge has helped save hundreds of families and individuals across the globe.

Personal Acknowledgments and Guidance Notes

What you just read actually happened. It was a real event that took place in 1992. For decades, events similiar to this one, have occurred across the globe, but very little have hit the headlines. I decided to write this account as a means of awareness to others, to take heed of the implications and dangers of dealing with dark forces with limited or no previous experience. It has taken me over twenty years of studying and practical experience, to be able to work with, and deal with, forces far more sinister and malevolent than your typical residual energies.

Thankfully, over the years, I have worked with many professional paranormal groups who have extensive, practical and theoretical knowledge, to be able to handle darker cases of hauntings. I have close relations with several teams, both here in my native United Kingdom and in the United States. I have listed at the end of this acknowledgment, a guideline and contact page of reliable resources that I personally recommend, if you, as the reader, feel you require professional help with your problem.

At the end of the day, take my advice. If you feel you are dealing with something that is dark, malevolent or indeed, potentially demonic, ***Do not attempt to deal with it***

Leave it for those who have the experience!

Personal thanks

I would like to personally thank the following people for their endless support in my venture and to their highly recommended professional services.

Dana and Chris Wingerd (Founders of Phenemenology Conventions)

Mike Cellar (Dark Cellar Productions)
www.darkcellarproductions.net

Robert & Sandra Bandov (Bearfort Paranormal)
www.bearfortparanormal.com

Lily Elkins (Hope Paranormal) www.hopeparanormal.org

Nick Lantz (Paranormal Author/Researcher) www.nlantz.com

Lora Shirey (FAITH Paranormal & Haldeman Mansions)
faithparanormal@yahoo.com

Eric Altman (Field Investigator) www.ericaltman.net

David Juliano OSM (Rev. Deliverance Minister)
www.sanctuarydeliverance.com

John Zaffis (Godfather of Paranormal) www.johnzaffis.com

Jan Murphy (UK Investigator) Facebook:
janmurphyparanormal.com

Mark Whyatt (Derby Paranormal Investigations) Facebook: D.P.I

Simon Bampfylde (British Paranormal Society)
www.britishparanormal.org.uk

Sean Cadman (Professional Investigator UK)
www.paraforceuk.com

Helen Davies (Investigator) www.southwalesghostwatch.co.uk

Robert & Deborah Best (Paranormal Team. PA)
www.chesterfieldparanormalresearch.com

Finally, a last quick personal thank you to my close friends; Bill Bean, Brian Cano, Steven LaChance, John Zaffis, Carmen Reed, and Matt Hall.

Printed in Great Britain
by Amazon

74332655R00051